Wild Water

Aqua Sports

BY S.L. HAMILTON

A&D Xtreme
An imprint of Abdo Publishing | www.abdopublishing.com

Visit us at
www.abdopublishing.com

Printed in the United States of America, North Mankato, Minnesota.
052015
092015

 PRINTED ON RECYCLED PAPER

Editor: John Hamilton
Graphic Design: Sue Hamilton
Cover Design: Sue Hamilton
Cover Photo: JetSurf
Interior Photos: AP-pgs 7, 10-11 & 22-23; Corbis-pg 6; Innespace Productions-pgs 16 & 17; iStock-pgs 14-15, 30-31 & 32; Jetavation-pgs 4-5 & 8-9; Jetsurf-pgs 1, 2-3 & 12-13; Schiller Sports-pgs 20-21; Seabob-pgs 24-25; Subwing-pgs 26-27; U-Boat Worx/David Pearlman-pgs 28 & 29, U.S. Coast Guard-pg 23 (insert), Waterpillar-pgs 18-19.

Websites
To learn more about Wild Water action, visit booklinks.abdopublishing.com. These links are routinely monitored and updated to provide the most current information available.

Library of Congress Control Number: 2015930946

Cataloging-in-Publication Data

Hamilton, S.L.
  Aqua sports / S.L. Hamilton.
   p. cm. -- (Wild water)
ISBN 978-1-62403-749-8
1. Aquatic sports--Juvenile literature.
2. Outdoor recreation--Juvenile literature.
I. Title.
797--dc23

2015930946

Contents

Aqua Sports

Aqua sports are water activities that get a person's heart racing with fun exercise and adventures. These cool activities may be above the water, on the water, or underwater.

Some aqua sports require practice and skills. Others call for balance, muscle, and the ability to swim. Some sports use today's most high-tech equipment. Others make use of traditional watercraft. All are wild-water fun!

XTREME FACT – It is estimated that less than half the people in the world can swim.

Jetpacks

Jetpacks seem like science fiction, but today they are used to fly above the water. The Aquaflyer and Jetlev-Flyer use powerful streams of water from personal watercraft to send riders soaring into the air. People learn to takeoff, fly, turn, hover, and land with their jetpacks. Skilled riders can even dive underwater and come back up!

***XTREME FACT* – A water-driven jetpack allows a rider to go up to 33 feet (10 m) in the air.**

Jetovators

The Jetovator is like riding a motorcycle over the water. The Jetovator's hose attaches to a personal watercraft (PWC). The PWC sends powerful jet streams of water up through the 40-foot (12-m) hose, blasting the vehicle and rider into the air.

XTREME FACT – Riders can reach speeds of 25 mph (40 kpm) on the Jetovator.

Riders control the Jetovator's height, speed, and direction. They can push it into backflips, barrel rolls, or corkscrews. The Jetovator can rocket up to 25 feet (8 m) in the air or dive 10 feet (3 m) underwater.

Flyboards

Flyboards propel riders using two jet streams of water. The water is funneled through a hose attached to a personal watercraft (PWC). The thrust of the PWC powers the Flyboard.

Flyboard

The tilt of the athlete's feet determines the Flyboard's direction. Flyboarders may soar into the air, twisting, turning, and somersaulting. Or they may drop down, torpedoing below the water's surface. People who know how to dive, ski, and snowboard often become skilled Flyboarders.

XTREME FACT – Flyboarding is also known as "surfing the sky."

Power Boards

JetSurf is a motorized power board used to race or surf. A handheld controller allows the surfer to accelerate to jump, perform tricks, or race across the waves. Surfing skills, wave knowledge, and balance are assisted with the JetSurf's powerful engine.

XTREME QUOTE – *"It looked in-between a Formula One-ish car and a Jet Ski."*
–*Kai Lenny, surfer on the JetSurf*

Dragon Boat Racing

Dragon boat racing originated in China about 2,400 years ago. Today, the excitement has spread from Asia to more than 60 countries. Outside of Asia, major dragon boat races are held in Sweden, the United States, and Canada.

XTREME FACT – Dragon boats are sleek and beautiful. They are usually 40 feet (12 m) in length, but only 4 feet (1.2 m) wide.

Dragon boats vary in size and the number of people on a team. Typically, it is a 22-person team made up of a sweep or steerer (back), plus one drummer (front), who beats a rhythm for the 20 paddlers. Races are straight sprints, usually 500 meters (1,640 feet) in length. Coordinated rowing, strength, and stamina make for a winning dragon boat team.

Seabreachers

Seabreacher is a cross between a speed boat, a submarine, a personal watercraft, and a whale. As the name says, pilots have the unique ability to make the vehicle rise up and out of the water, or "breach" the surface. The vehicles are painted in many different designs.

Seabreacher with outside passenger.

Seabreachers can race across the water at speeds up to 55 mph (89 kph).

As a submersible, Seabreachers can dive 5 feet (1.5 m) down at 20 mph (32 kph).

Seabreachers can jump 20 feet (6 m) out of the water. Some can even do 360° barrel rolls!

Waterpillars

Waterpillar riders need strong legs and a sense of fun. The water vehicle can be pedaled by one or two riders. Each giant wheel is 7 feet (2.1 m) in diameter.

The Waterpillar can be run on saltwater or freshwater. Riders may pedal across calm water or waves.

One rider controls the steering. By pressing the left or right hand levers, the matching wheel stops. The opposite wheel keeps moving, allowing the Waterpillar to make sharp turns.

XTREME FACT – The entire Waterpillar pedal boat is 8 feet (2.4 m) wide.

Water Bikes

Schiller water bikes let riders pedal across the water just as bicyclists do on land. However, water bike riders don't have to deal with traffic and people. To start out, riders inflate the two pontoons and assemble the bike. Once on the water, pumping the pedals operates the bike's underwater propeller. Handlebars steer the bike by moving the rudder. Riders can pedal the bike at a swift 8 knots (9 mph / 15 kph).

XTREME FACT – *Unlike people in kayaks or canoes, the Schiller water bike lets riders sit up above the water. This position gives a better view of their surroundings.*

XTREME QUOTE – *"I had the X1 (water bike) out at the beach locally, about a mile offshore, and ended up biking with dolphins."*

–Judah Schiller, founder Schiller Sports

Water Rollers

It's a cross between a gerbil ball and a glass bottom boat! Water rollers are giant plastic balls that let riders walk, run, or crawl on top of the water. Athletes are zipped inside the watertight ball. A standard 10-minute ride gets the heart pumping and gives people a cool view of the marine life below.

XTREME FACT – *In 2014, marathoner Reza Baluchi tried to run from Florida to Bermuda in a hydro pod. After 4 days on the Atlantic Ocean, he was rescued by the Coast Guard when he became disoriented and dehydrated.*

Water Scooters

The Seabob water scooter lets riders race across the water's surface or the ocean floor. Strong arm muscles and the ability to hold one's breath are needed as riders power through the water. Riders lean left or right, applying a light pressure to control the scooter's direction.

XTREME FACT – A Seabob glides at low speed or races up to 12 miles per hour (20 kph) above the water and 9 mph (15 kph) underwater. It can dive as deep as 131 feet (40 m). A safety device can be programmed to keep a rider from diving too deep.

Subwings

The Subwing lets a diver move up and down or take a thrilling spin underwater. The Subwing is pulled by a rope attached to a boat. Riders control their depth by tilting the two connected wings at different angles.

Typically, a person will be underwater for about 10-15 seconds and will dive down about 10 feet (3 m) using the Subwing. Experienced divers can use the rear grip to hold on with one hand, equalize the pressure in their ears, and, with a longer rope, go down deeper.

Sport Subs

C-Quester is a battery powered sport sub that brings underwater exploration to adventurers. Created by U-Boat Worx of the Netherlands, this submersible has an acrylic and steel 360-degree viewport that allows two or three riders to look all around.

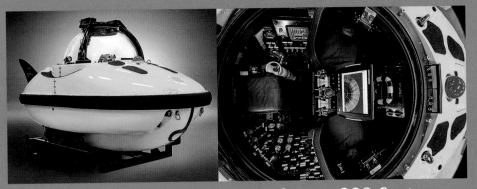

The C-Quester dives down as far as 328 feet (100 m), and can operate for up to eight hours. On the surface, it can go as fast as 4 knots (4.6 mph/7.4 kph). Its underwater speed is 2 knots (2.3 mph/3.7 kph). One of the most adventurous water vehicles made, this sport sub opens up the world's seas and oceans to explorers of all ages.

Glossary

BREACH

When fish or an underwater craft jump out of the water.

CORKSCREW

To move in a spiraling motion.

DEHYDRATE

Extreme loss of water from the body, often because no water is available, or because of an illness or intense exercise.

DIAMETER

The measurement of a straight line passing through an object from one side to the other.

diameter

FRESHWATER

Water sources with little amounts of salt in them, such as lakes and rivers. Saltwater, such as water in oceans and seas, has a higher salt content.

KNOT

A unit of speed equaling one nautical mile per hour. One nautical mile per hour is equal to 1.151 miles per hour or 1.852 kilometers per hour.

Personal Watercraft (PWC)

A water vehicle mainly designed for individual use. PWCs are used for play, transportation, and racing. They are often known by the manufacturers's names: Jet Ski, Sea-Doo, and Waverunner.

Pontoons

Hollow floating objects, sometimes inflatable, that are used on such things as sea planes or floating bikes. Pontoons allow an object to float.

Saltwater

Water with a heavier salt content than freshwater, about 35 parts per thousand. It is found in Earth's seas and oceans.

Science Fiction

A type of fiction that involves the future and advancements in science. This may include stories about flying with jetpacks, time travel, or robots. Many science fiction ideas of the past have become reality today.

Submersible

Another name for a submarine.

Index